THE BASIC HANDBOOK
OF FIGURE DRAWING

Students, professional artists, Sunday painters—
here is the definitive book on the basic principles
and techniques of fine figure drawing.

JOHN R. GRABACH, the author and illus-
trator, has taught life drawing, figure and
landscape painting for twenty years at
The School of Industrial and Fine Arts in
Newark, New Jersey.

HENRY GASSER, who wrote the Introduction, is the author of the successful *How
to Draw and Paint,* also published by
Dell.

HOW TO DRAW THE HUMAN FIGURE

by JOHN R. GRABACH

with an Introduction by HENRY GASSER

Published by
DELL PUBLISHING CO., INC.
750 Third Avenue
New York, N.Y. 10017

Photographs by Jackson O'Sullivan

The author acknowledges the assistance of Stephen Haff.

Dedicated to: GWYNNE LENNON

First printing—August, 1958
Second printing—November, 1958
Third printing—August, 1959
Fourth printing—March, 1963
Fifth printing—March, 1967
Sixth printing—July, 1969

B-383

Printed in U.S.A.

INTRODUCTION

It was my good fortune to have had John Grabach as my teacher. Years later, our happy association was renewed when I became Director of the Newark School of Fine and Industrial Arts where Grabach was the head of the Drawing Department. During his twenty-five years on the faculty he has taught drawing and painting to more than four thousand students. A superb draftsman, he possesses also that priceless attribute of every really good teacher—the ability to inspire his students.

Today, when "isms" flourish and drawing is often considered secondary, Grabach is a reassuring landmark to students seeking a meaningful path in the multi-directional world of art. He stresses the fact that time spent in drawing the living figure is never lost. In this book he sets forth his sound principles of good drawing, constantly emphasizing the importance of the search for the key line. It is the knowledge of this line in the drawing of the figure, he points out, that gives a vigorous strength to the structure of the drawing. The key line may be straight, convex, or triangular. A line that may appear to be concave will be visualized by the artist as though it were composed of a number of convex or straight lines.

Throughout the book, Grabach analyzes each drawing to show the key-line foundation. Once this is determined, the realization of the volumes that create the form follows, always looking for the big masses or shapes. Only when all this has been put on paper are the details added.

While the student should not limit himself to one medium, charcoal is the most versatile of these. It is particularly adapted to making drawings with tonal qualities ranging from the palest gray to the most velvet of blacks. Charcoal is unsurpassed for preliminary sketches and studies for subsequent paintings.

If the student has acquired a slovenly manner of working, slurring over difficult passages, Grabach recommends drawing with a lead pencil of not too soft a quality as a means of acquiring discipline. His chapter on silver point and pencil drawing gives an excellent approach to this medium.

Generous space is given to anatomy from the artistic point of view, and to the drawing of drapery. Too frequently this latter subject has been neglected. The influence of the underlying figure on the drapery is shown with excellent renderings, again employing the key line in determining the folds of various materials.

The section on painting is presented in color and shows step-by-step guidance from the painting of simple monochromatic studies to the use of full color.

With a bare minimum of text (a gratifying accomplishment for any artist) Grabach has created a book that I am confident will be of inestimable assistance to those who are seriously interested in improving their mastery of drawing and painting.

HENRY M. GASSER, N.A.

THE ART OF DRAWING
FROM THE FIGURE

Art is to be found in all objects, the ordinary and unpleasant as well as the strange and the beautiful. We consider the rose a thing of beauty, but not the toad; yet the toad has in its appearance potentialities for artistic invention as much as has the rose—perhaps more, because it is less static.

Art is the artist's expression of delight in what he sees, and his attempt to communicate that feeling to others. As a means of expression it is infinitely varied. The student may express his art in any number of styles, and still work within the realm of today's art.

Differing states of the public mind lead to the emphasis of different styles of art at various periods, but there is no era, except one of utter decay, in which sound draftsmanship will not be recognized. Because representation of the human figure is the most difficult of all drawing, the artist who can draw figures well is necessarily more skilled than those who do other subjects.

Accurate drawing is not copying the model, as if one were a photographer. Mechanical copying of a figure is rigid, satisfying neither the artist nor the observer. Instead, one should draw freely, with enthusiasm, exercising the faculties of interpretation and expression. The superior draftsman is never indifferent to his subject. Development of his ability to express and interpret will continually give him greater power.

In working from the figure, the artist must be in the main a realist. Though outward understanding of appearances cannot be his only goal, he still must be able to render those appearances, to express their substance, to represent softness and hardness, lines and masses, design, and the interrelationship of the whole.

The best progress in drawing the figure can be made by use of the living model; no other subject yields as much practical experience. Drawing from the living model will develop force in handling, enlarge one's capacity for interpretation, and continually add to one's knowledge of the figure. From the living model one can get the most highly idealized of all artistic expressions.

Drawing can be a vast and many-sided performance or a shallow affair, depending on how much the artist sees in the figure and how well he can express it. The true draftsman applies all his will and energy to the work, concentrating his entire attention on the subject and seeking to express everything that can be represented. His precise and accurate rendering must express through line, form and rhythm the variety of tones created by light and shade, volume, substance and texture, and must translate color values into black and white. More, the true draftsman will seek to express the inner meaning, the very soul of the subject.

Line, form and rhythm are all of vital importance, and their handling is an essential part of what this book endeavors to impart. How much can be expressed in the simple line is shown by the figures ornamenting the best Greek vases.

Delineation, that is, representation through the use of the simple line, differs absolutely from the method used by the masters of the Renaissance. The Renaissance masters used the most rapid means of expression, indicating shading by sure but rude means, a few hasty strokes of charcoal or crayon. They caught the form, but paid no attention to the outline that is so essential in delineation.

Rhythm is produced by the interplay of fast and slow lines, stiff and flowing lines, strong and weak lines, and of forms, all in proper relationship to the subject. A straight line is fast, while a helical line, resembling a coiled spring, is slow. The more one stretches out the spring the faster the line; the more closely it is coiled the slower the line. This is because the eye moves faster over a straight line than over a curved one, and the more complex the curvature the more slowly the eye moves. (See "Speed of Line," page 30.)

In drawing textures and substances the use of lines of varying speeds is essential. For instance, thin drapery will have faster lines than heavier material. Surfaces can be expressed by placing many lines together. Contrast emphasizes and heightens the effect of various lines. A stiff line seems doubly stiff when next to a flowing line. A slight curve becomes more pronounced when placed beside a straight line. Good artists make use of the principle of contrast, and both the most delicate grace and the sturdiest strength are derived from observance of this principle.

Form, outline and rhythm are all made clear in this volume, so that the reader can obtain a summary of the whole with strict reference to the time at his disposal. This gives more latitude to originality and allows freer play for personal qualities in one's drawings. It will lead to the bold exaggeration of strength which is a part of artistic expression, giving emphasis to the drawing and a strong spirit, an individual accent to the work.

No important principle can be ignored in drawing the figure, but when a student sees detail too clearly he is often led into excessive analysis. In this dangerous, if not fatal, state he perceives detail that he should not express. He is blinded to the larger masses that are the primary key to successful interpretation. He draws an aggregation of fragments instead of the whole, like one who is so busy counting leaves he cannot see the shape of the tree.

The artist can only express light and dark in proper proportion by controlling each shade in relation to the whole. As the light and dark in drawing must be relative, they are translated synthetically from the actual light and darkness perceived on the model. Students will help their work if they use artificial lighting of the figure to concentrate the scattered forms into large planes, binding all the fragments together. The arrangement of good forms is strikingly apparent in first rate figure drawing, and arrangement is one of the distinctions separating good drawing from the mechanical or mediocre. It should be realized, too, that contrasting forms modify each other, just as contrasting lines do.

9

It is well for the artist to study anatomy, as the increased knowledge of the muscular structure of the body will assist in correct modeling. To model or shade each part so that it stands out or recedes in correct proportion to each other part of the whole is an essential part of drawing. The projection of each form must be expressed in correct relationship to all other projecting parts.

The eyes, at their best, see things all together in their correct relationship. Artists are strong as they adhere to such perception, weak in direct proportion to their failure to see the whole. Understanding is the prime requisite, with good eyes and skillful fingers next in importance. Individual temperament has much to do with an artist's product, which is so peculiarly the product of an individual. The necessary concentration of one's faculties on one subject over a long period of time comes easily to some, while to others it proves virtually impossible.

BEGINNING THE DRAWING

Before you start your drawing get a clear conception of the figure before you. Study the model from different angles. Understand what the figure is doing and the nature of the action. This will be the real beginning of your drawing.

Have the drawing board straight up and down. Sit away from it at arm's length. Give your arm full play, so that you can draw from the shoulder and get freedom in your line. Start about an inch from the top of the paper, and draw from the top down to an inch from the bottom. Do not get too far away from the model. If you do, you will miss the fine gradations of the form. See that you have a good light on your paper and a strong, direct light on the model. A diffused light fails to tie the forms and masses together, leaving too many fragmentary details.

Start with the head; it gives the scale for your drawing. With the head drawn in first you can get the proper proportions for the rest of the body. It is wrong to try to place the head on the body after the torso is drawn. Some students have acquired this habit, and once adopted it is hard to break.

Be careful not to place the model in a strained pose that cannot be held for twenty minutes at a time. Various marks can be noted on the figure that will guide you in making correct measurements. Place the model on the stand so that the center of the figure will be at eye level, giving some perspective with an arch. In making measurements, extend the arm straight out, and keep your eye as close as possible to the shoulder. Use your charcoal stick to register correctly each space you want to measure. With practice you will become extremely accurate in judging angles and proportions.

Do not depend on the kneaded eraser for lights. The eraser should only be used to get the sharp lights where muscles go over or under each other. If it is used to obtain the light masses the drawing will be chalky. Let the paper make all the lights possible.

Knead the eraser between two fingers until it has a sharp edge, which is the only part that should be used. Rub as little as you can with the eraser for too much rubbing will kill the surface of the paper. Use the hand and fingers to form your shading. In very small parts of the figure, such as the head or hands, the stump can be used, but on all larger surfaces the hand will produce the best effects.

Some charcoal will not stay on the paper as well as it should. If that should happen, it is best to try another stick of charcoal. In time one learns to pick out good charcoal. If you rub over the charcoal and it has a soft, smooth, silky feeling, you can be sure that it is a desirable stick.

The value of charcoal as a medium is its distinctive characteristic ability to fill in the broad masses of shadows rapidly, and the luminous quality of shadows and delicacy of halftones it produces. It is the first of all media, offering the greatest freedom of use and effect, limited only by the ability of the artist to use it.

Don't be desultory in your work. Once you start your drawing, stick to it. The drawing of the figure is difficult, but becomes so fascinating that a student captivated by it finds it hard to stay away from figure drawing.

If you are located where there is no school that has a figure class, get together a few congenial friends with an interest in drawing. Models can be obtained without too much difficulty, and use of this book will provide reference material that should suit anyone's needs.

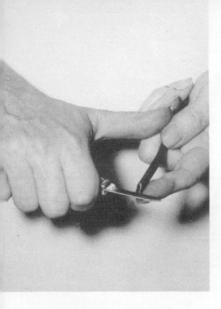

The Charcoal

Material used in charcoal drawing includes soft, medium and hard sticks of charcoal, a drawing board 19 by 25 inches, Michelangelo* white charcoal paper (or a similarly good grade), charcoal fixative, an atomizer, or convenient Tuffilm ™* Spray Fixative in pressurized spray can, a large rag, stumps, and a kneaded eraser.

*Trademark of
M. Grumbacher, Inc.

To sharpen charcoal draw the knife toward you. This keeps the point from breaking.

The thumb is used to produce roundness, and gives a splendid texture to the charcoal.

This plate shows the
use of the side
of the hand in shading
charcoal. The back of
the hand is used
for a large
surface for getting
breadth and roundness.

To remove any
part of the drawing
do not rub,
but dust off the
drawing with the rag.

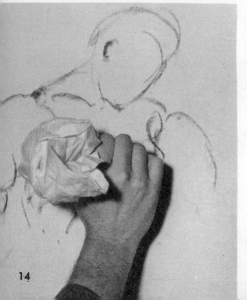

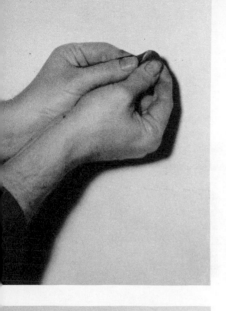

The Kneaded Eraser

Knead the eraser
with the two fingers to
a sharp thin edge.

The eraser pressed or
kneaded into a sharp edge
is used to create
a sharp light line
accenting and modifying
a form.

The Knife

Use the back
of the pocket knife to
shade small parts
of the drawing, parts
that are too small
for use of
the fingers. The
knife will give a fine
tonal modulation
to the small forms.

The Stump

To shade
and round small
forms.

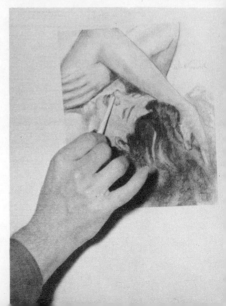

PLACING THE FIGURE

Placing the figure too far to the right of paper and too low.

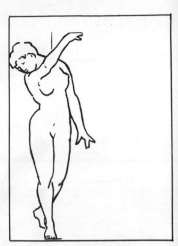

Too far to the left of paper and too low.

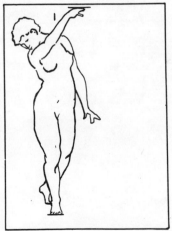

Too high and too far to the left ot paper.

Correctly placed on the paper. Notice the space at the top and bottom of the figure. 17

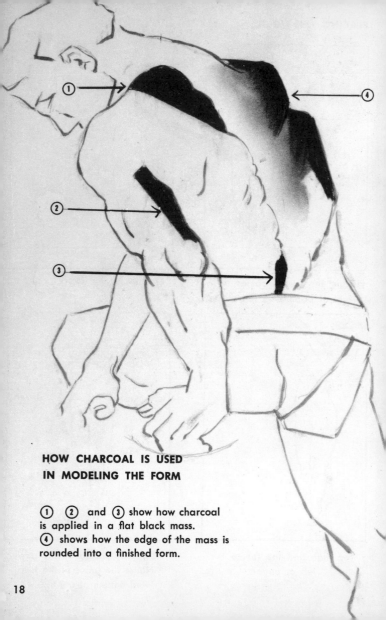

HOW CHARCOAL IS USED
IN MODELING THE FORM

① ② and ③ show how charcoal
is applied in a flat black mass.
④ shows how the edge of the mass is
rounded into a finished form.

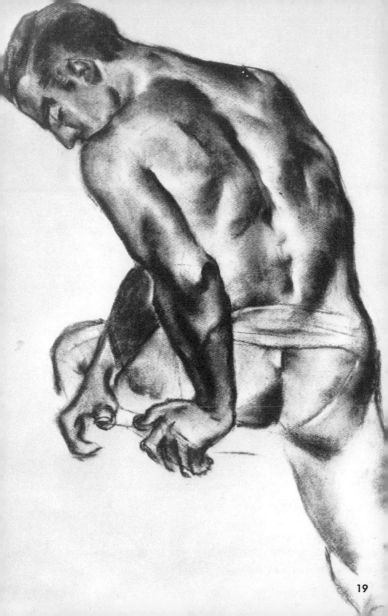

19

The most delicate grays
to velvety black
can be produced with charcoal.

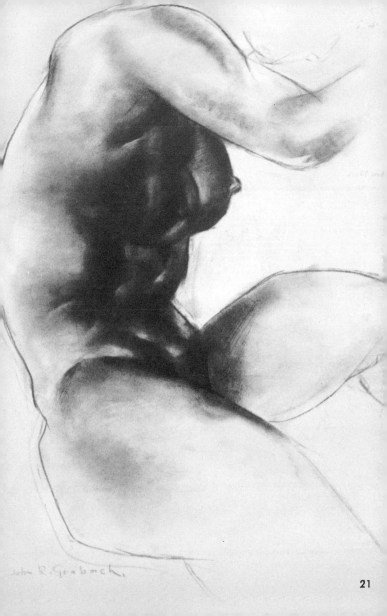

John R. Grabach

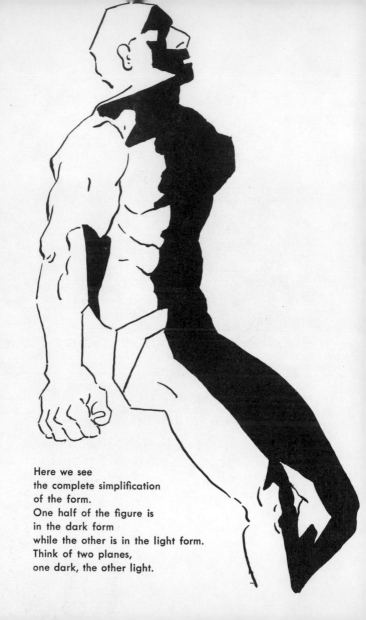

Here we see
the complete simplification
of the form.
One half of the figure is
in the dark form
while the other is in the light form.
Think of two planes,
one dark, the other light.

23

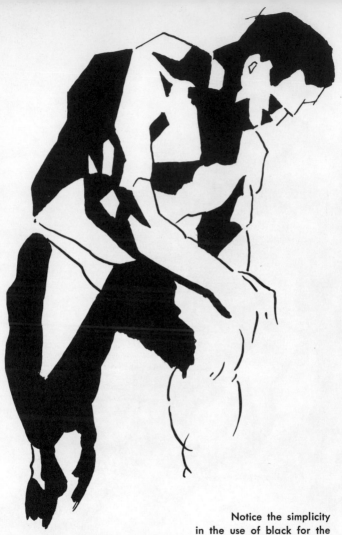

Notice the simplicity
in the use of black for the
heavy shadows. The interesting
surface is then modeled into the form.
(The model was in a very strong light.)

John R Grobach

THE QUICK SKETCH

The drawing on the opposite page
was made in five minutes.
It was made with heavy, soft charcoal,
about one-quarter of
an inch thick. It was
twice the size of the reproduction,
but quick sketches can be
made very much smaller.
The quick sketch is possibly
the best training for the student.
In such work as this,
the student will
cultivate a rapid memory.
It also gives an easy
feeling to the drawing,
as well as a free rhythm.
Try to make a sketch
in say two or three minutes,
and from as many angles as possible.
Quick sketching is to the artist
what practicing scales is to the musician.

Five minute sketch

Three-minute sketch

Five-minute sketch

SPEED OF LINE

Drawing is a combination of fast and slow lines.
The straight line is fast; the sharper the curve,
the slower the line movement.

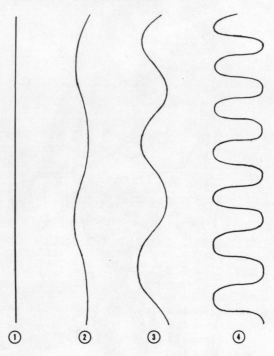

① Fast line.

② A little slower line.

③ Much slower line.

④ Very slow line.

HOW THE KEY LINE IS USED

Straight line opposite curved line.

Straight line with curved line above.

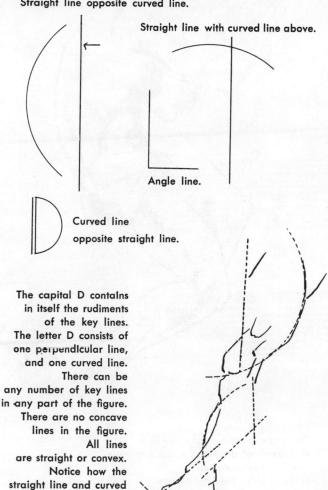

Angle line.

Curved line
opposite straight line.

The capital D contains
in itself the rudiments
of the key lines.
The letter D consists of
one perpendicular line,
and one curved line.
There can be
any number of key lines
in any part of the figure.
There are no concave
lines in the figure.
All lines
are straight or convex.
Notice how the
straight line and curved
line are used.

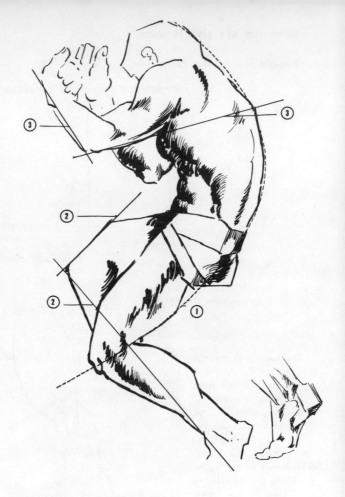

The angle is used as one key line.
First sketch of drawing on opposite page.
The key lines were used
in the order of their importance.
The first line used
on this drawing was key line no. ①

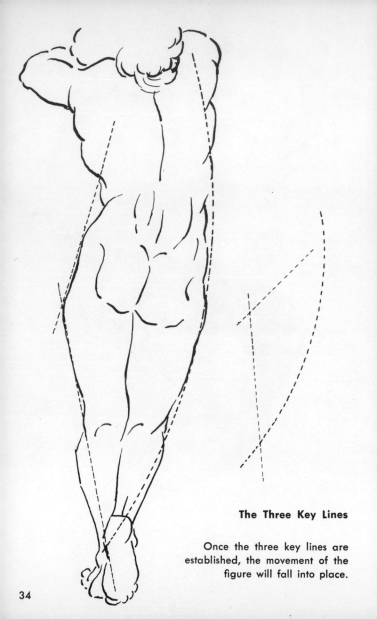

The Three Key Lines

Once the three key lines are established, the movement of the figure will fall into place.

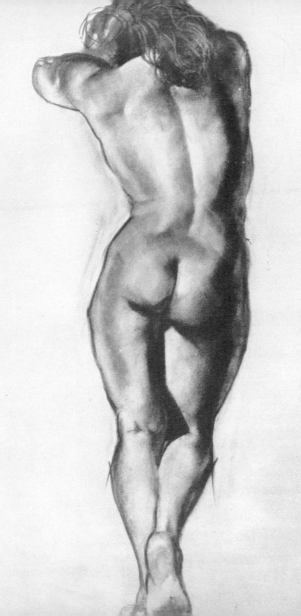

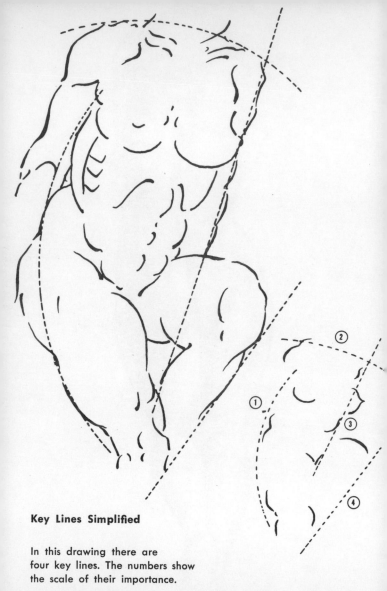

Key Lines Simplified

In this drawing there are
four key lines. The numbers show
the scale of their importance.

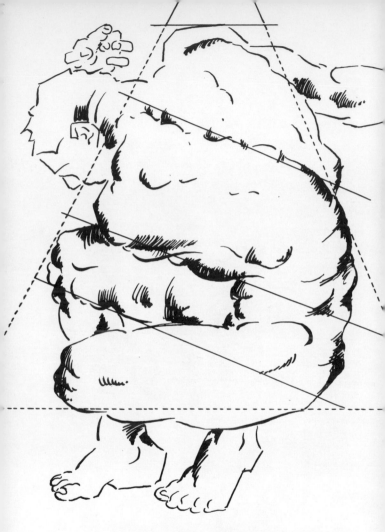

Crouching figure in the shape of the pyramid, with lines limited by points, surfaces limited by line, and the solid limited by surfaces. All surfaces are in relationship to each other. The substance of the figure is held throughout to the pyramid.

John C. Grabach

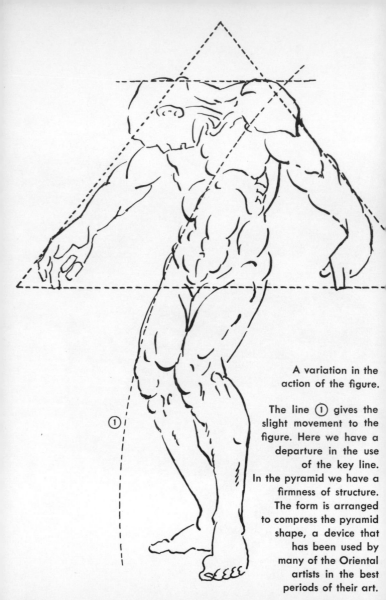

A variation in the
action of the figure.

The line ① gives the
slight movement to the
figure. Here we have a
departure in the use
of the key line.
In the pyramid we have a
firmness of structure.
The form is arranged
to compress the pyramid
shape, a device that
has been used by
many of the Oriental
artists in the best
periods of their art.

Locate key lines
in this
drawing.

41

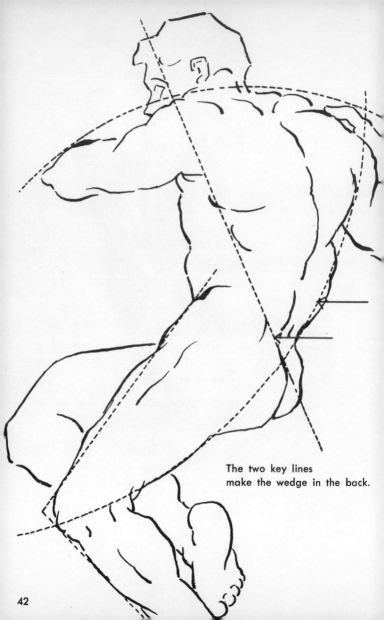

The two key lines
make the wedge in the back.

Locate use of
wedge in this drawing.

43

The key lines are used to
give a feeling of speed of movement
as well as structural division.
This principle was
employed by the Greek sculptors.

44

John R. Grabach

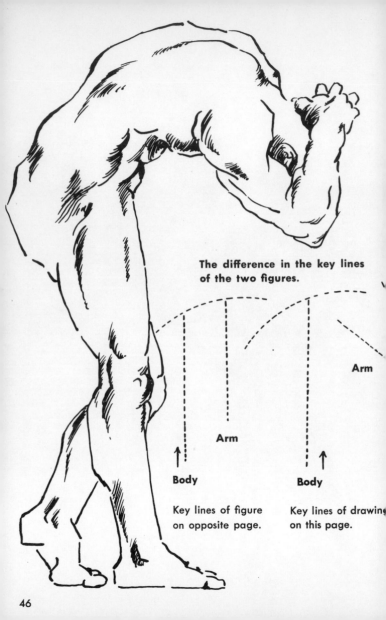

**The difference in the key lines
of the two figures.**

Arm

Arm

Body

Body

Key lines of figure
on opposite page.

Key lines of drawing
on this page.

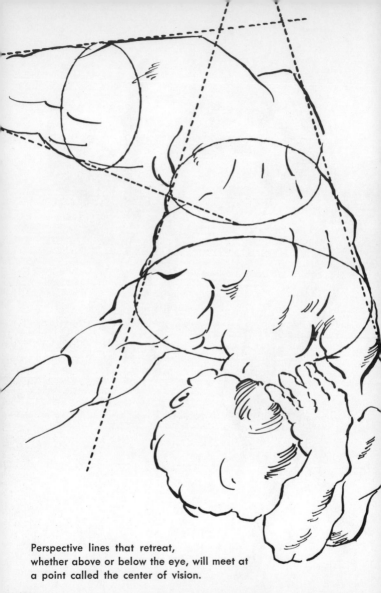

Perspective lines that retreat,
whether above or below the eye, will meet at
a point called the center of vision.

In this drawing the structure
has been built up by the
use of the circle. On the torso
the complete circle has
been used to make the foreshortening.
Notice the rhythm in the design.

In this figure the circle and oval have been used to get the structure, and the three key lines to get the rhythm of design or action.

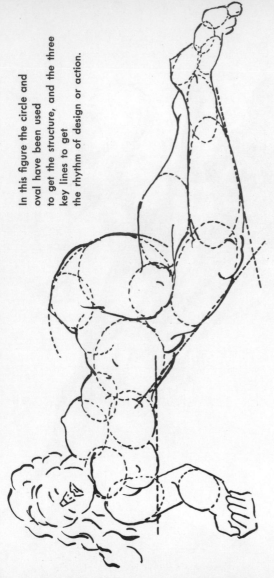

53

In this drawing we see the figure
in an easy pose, with simple lines. The figure
is constructed in circles and ovals.

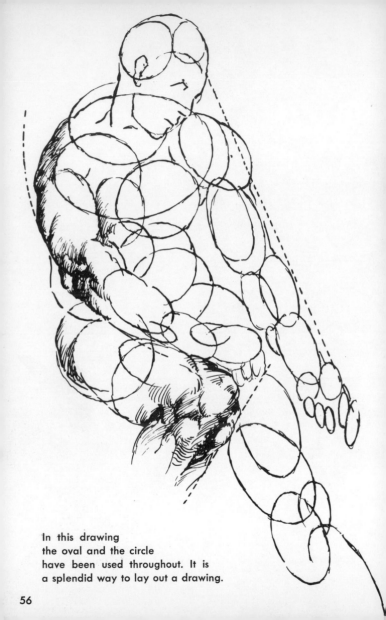

In this drawing
the oval and the circle
have been used throughout. It is
a splendid way to lay out a drawing.

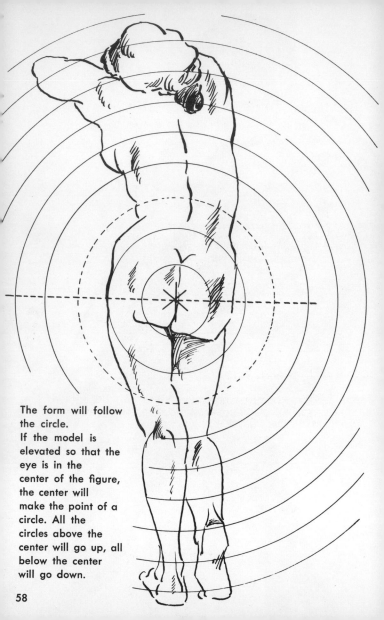

The form will follow the circle.
If the model is elevated so that the eye is in the center of the figure, the center will make the point of a circle. All the circles above the center will go up, all below the center will go down.

58

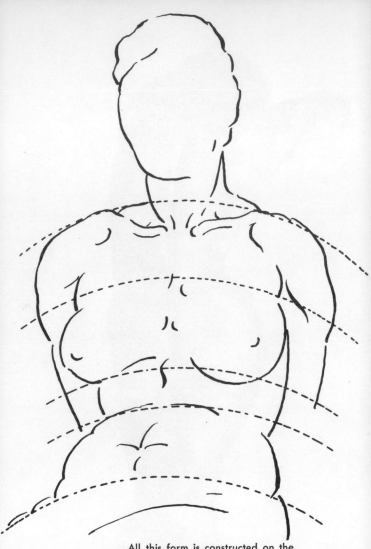

All this form is constructed on the
circle, which produces a perspective
that causes the torso to lean back.

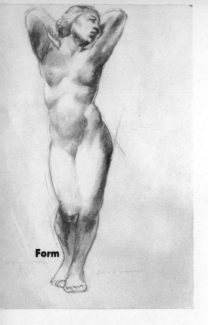

Form

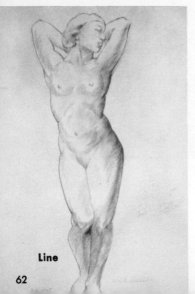

Line

THE PAINTER'S
APPROACH

In the painter's approach the
line is a result of
developing the form.
He sees shape,
then form.
To make it more clear,
let us say the head
is egg-shaped,
and the eyes, nose,
mouth, and ears
are the form in the shape.
The principle is
to see all shape,
then form, and line last.
In drawing hair
we see the shape, then
develop the small
strands of the hair.

AN INTRODUCTION
TO OIL PAINTING

The palette is best arranged systematically—on the left side the Thalo®* Blue, French Ultramarine, Burnt Sienna, Yellow Ochre and Alizarin Crimson, Golden; in the center Zinc White, next to the White on the right, either Vermilion or Cadmium Red, Light; next Viridian and then Lemon Yellow and Cadmium Yellow, Light. Use a purified linseed oil; turpentine alone is not recommended since it reduces the brilliancy of the color. Some artists use a 50-50 mixture of linseed oil and turpentine.** It retains the brilliancy, adds fluidity, and does not slow the drying as does 100% linseed or poppyseed oil. For general painting the color should be applied with a reasonably heavily loaded brush and a minimum amount of oil. Use linen or a good grade of cotton canvas or canvas board. The grain of the canvas is a matter of preference. Too absorbent a ground is not recommended.

Start drawing with charcoal. When the drawing is satisfactory, apply a fixative to keep it from mixing with the colors. It is always best to use an easel, inclined forward to prevent shine or reflected light from striking the canvas. The easel can be a studio type or a portable one, such as those used for outdoor sketching. The palette is usually either oval or square. Once your palette has been arranged, retain the sequence of colors for future work. Heavy, dry paint can be scraped off with the palette knife, which should have a pliable blade. This knife is used as well for arranging color and mixing tints. With some painters it takes the place of a brush when applying color.

Use the brush as much as possible. Most painters prefer brushes made of white hog hair bristle. Flat brushes with short bristle hair are called "Brights" and are generally pre-

* ®Registered Trademark, M. Grumbacher, Inc.
**Grumtine TM (Pat. Pending) is an organic solvent used for all painting purposes. It is superior to turpentine.

ferred, though for some purposes "Rounds" are useful. "Flats" are brushes which have the "Brights" shape but with long bristle. Red sable brushes which have the same shape as bristle brushes are useful for blending of areas and for glazing. After use, brushes should be washed with Grumtine ™* or turpentine and then with mild hand soap. Stroke the brush on the soap and work up a lather on the palm of the hand. Repeat the process with occasional rinses until no color remains in the brush. Use a lukewarm-to-cold water and press the hairs of the brush back into the original shape. A brush in which the color has been allowed to dry is difficult to clean and is permanently damaged.

A mahl-stick can be used to steady the hand while painting details. A conveniently hung mirror will prove useful too. It enables the artist to detect faults in drawing which he may otherwise fail to observe.

Buy the best colors you can afford, and use only those that are permanent. The color chart of a reliable manufacturer will give the key to permanency.

Learn as much as you can about mixing colors to obtain new combinations from the palette. You may then add a new color to your palette in order to increase your color range. Eliminate a color when you discover a substitute that is more pleasing to you. Do not limit your experimenting, but exhaust all the possibilities of each color before adding a new one to your palette.

For example: while Zinc White is vital to my permanent palette, I have recently experimented with MG® White,** which is especially made for rapid drying. I find it excellent for underpainting and for all texture-impasto techniques. I now supplement my Zinc White with this new MG® White.** Alizarin Crimson, Golden is another recent addition. Unlike the regular Alizarin Crimson which has a purple cast when mixed with white, Alizarin Crimson, Golden retains the vital red hue and gives a beautiful rosy effect.

*Manufactured by M. Grumbacher, Inc.
**MG® White is a titanium white for textured underpainting and direct painting. Dries rapidly (2 to 4 hours) in moderate thickness. Made only by M. Grumbacher, Inc.

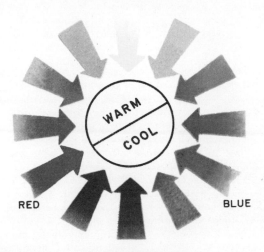

YELLOW

WARM
COOL

RED   BLUE

Color Chart courtesy of M. Grumbacher, Inc.
Brushes • Colors • Artists' Material

Technically, any color can be made by mixing the primary colors, yellow, red, and blue. Each of the secondary colors, orange, violet, and green, is made by mixing the two primary colors on either side of it.

Mixing primary and secondary colors produces the intermediate colors, yellow-orange, red-orange, red-violet, blue-violet, blue-green, and yellow-green.

The complement of each color is directly opposite it. Mixtures of complements make grays.

Colors containing a greater proportion of yellow or red are considered "warm." Conversely, colors containing a greater proportion of blue are "cool."

COLOR-MIXING

A. The three primary colors, yellow, red, and blue, mixed together neutralize each other to make a gray.

B. The three secondary colors, orange, violet, and green, mixed together neutralize each other to make a gray.

C. Two primary colors, in this case yellow and red, mixed together make a secondary color (orange).

D. Two primary colors, in this case blue and yellow, mixed together make a secondary color (green).

E. A primary color (yellow) mixed with a secondary color (green) makes an intermediate hue (yellow-green).

F. Two primary colors, in this case red and blue, mixed together make a secondary color (violet).

G. Two colors opposite each other on the color wheel (complementary colors) mixed together neutralize each other to make a gray. In this case yellow and violet were mixed to produce a gray.

H. When black is mixed with a color, it grays the color to produce a neutralized hue. In this case black was added to red to make a neutralized red.

I. When a neutralized color is mixed with a color, it grays the color to produce a neutralized hue. In this case a deep brown was added to blue to make a neutralized blue.

J. Here is another neutralized color mixed with a color to produce a neutralized hue. In this case a reddish brown was added to violet to make a neutralized violet.

The color chart illustrating the above mixtures was executed with water color. However, by simply adding white paint to each color the same results are obtained with oil paints.

Color Chart courtesy of M. Grumbacher, Inc.
Brushes ● Colors ● Artists' Material

Color-Mixing Exercises

Before working with the full range of your palette, you should familiarize yourself with the possibilities of each color.

An excellent start is to take a warm and a cool color and do a complete painting limiting yourself to these two colors. A good combination is Cobalt Blue and Burnt Sienna or French Ultramarine and Burnt Umber. You can use water color or oil; for the latter, white paint must be added. Improvise a landscape or build one from an outdoor sketch that you may have on hand. With blue as the cool color and brown as the warm, begin to paint the picture.

In some areas you will use the colors pure; in others, they will be combined. You will be amazed at the number of color variations that can be achieved with so simple a palette. Most important, you will discover the numerous shades of warm and cool grays that are obtainable.

For the next exercise, use three colors and explore their possibilities. Cobalt Blue, Light Red, and Yellow Ochre should allow you plenty of scope compared to the two-color exercise. Again, add white paint if you use oils. By painting the same subject used before, you will more readily realize the added possibilities of a third color.

Experiment along these lines by making up your own limited color combinations. Add a fourth color, and so on, until you acquire a working knowledge of all the colors you plan to use on your palette.

One important point will become apparent: The fewer colors you use, the easier it is to obtain color harmony. Every time a new color is added the risk of creating discord is increased.

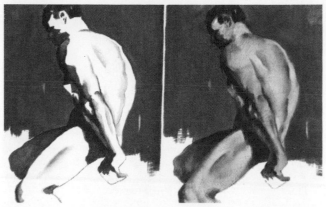

When starting to paint, limit the palette to a single color. You will discover that this approach will simplify the painting procedure. The illustrations on this page were painted with Burnt Sienna, an excellent color for such an approach. Note how only the main areas of light and dark are first indicated and then the halftones are added. This applies to whatever you paint. Devote much of your time to painting with a single color, experimenting not only with Burnt Sienna but Burnt Umber, Raw Umber, and so on. After you have learned something about the handling of one color it will be much easier to enlarge upon your palette.

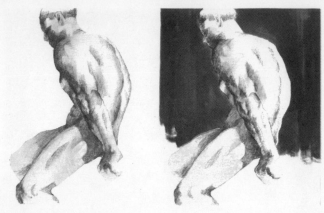

After a period of painting with a limited palette you can venture into painting in full color. Some time should be spent drawing in charcoal or pencil to indicate the division of light and shade and general arrangement. An approximate color of the background is then painted. This is followed by a rough indication of the shaded areas in the figure, using Burnt Sienna very thinly. In the final painting the color is applied in a heavier manner, imparting a substantial feeling to the entire picture. In your first full color paintings do not be too concerned about details—simplify and concentrate on the large masses.

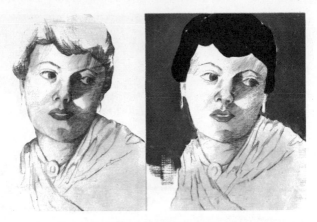

The basic principles of painting a head are shown in these four stages. First, a careful detailed drawing is made, depicting the arrangement of light and shade. Second, the background is painted. At the same time, the hair is painted to establish a dark note in relation to the background. In the third step, the shadowed areas are painted, leaving the white canvas to indicate the light areas. The fourth stage is devoted to the painting of the halftones. When the entire head area is covered with paint the highlights and accents are added, completing the portrait.

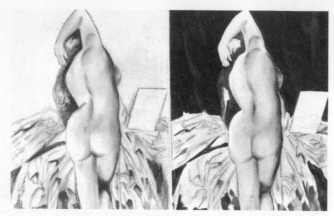

Glazing is the laying of thinly transparent color, diluted with your working medium, which allows the work beneath to appear through, tinged with the color of the glaze. The painting is advanced as far as possible with solid, opaque color. When dry, ground is glazed repeatedly with thinned, transparent color. The process is generally effected by the application of diluted, transparent color, but semi-transparent color is also used.

Scumbling resembles Glazing in that a very thin coat is lightly spread over portions of the work, but the color used is opaque instead of transparent.

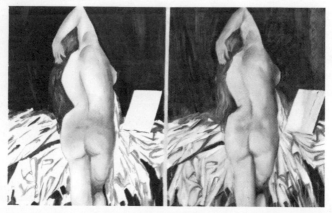

These plates illustrate the four steps for painting the head. *Above left.* Fully rendered drawing showing the form and indications of the shadows. *Above right.* First use of color after the drawing is made. Background is painted in first around head. Colors used are Burnt Sienna, Thalo* Blue and Yellow Ochre.

Below left. While background is still wet, head is painted with Burnt Sienna; all form is painted in. Background is brushed into shadow part to eliminate any cut-out look. *Below right.* In finishing the head, color is laid on with careful fusing and brought together into one unit. Head is completed in warm colors, with paint applied heavily.   * ® Reg. Trademark, M. Grumbacher, Inc.

Drawing is first made in charcoal with masses indicated. Start to paint by laying in background first, as illustrated above. Then lay in mass of figure, using Burnt Sienna and Thalo* Blue. Be careful not to use too much Thalo* Blue; it is a very strong color. Fuse tones with background, then lay in a middle tone with Yellow Ochre, White and some Burnt Sienna, a little Blue, as well as a very small amount of Alizarin Crimson, Golden. Follow most marked and characteristic accents of form of body. Model edges into background. Fuse tone into tone. When finished, use a deliberate touch to put in highlights.

* ® Reg. Trademark, M. Grumbacher, Inc.

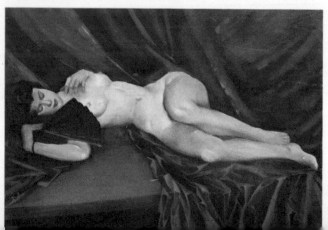

The head should be drawn slightly under life size. If it is drawn in actual size, the optical illusion will make the head look over life size. On the right is shown the procedure in painting the head, with the background painted first in Yellow Ochre, White, a small amount of Thalo* Blue and Burnt Sienna. For the coat, Prussian Blue, Yellow Ochre, Burnt Sienna and a very small amount of White is used to make the color opaque. As the painting progresses, warmer colors are added to the flesh area with Alizarin Crimson, Golden and Cadmium Red, Light being the principal colors used. The features are carefully rendered and the entire head area gradually refined. Accents of the ears, eyes, nostrils, and so on, are put in to complete the painting.

* ®Reg. Trademark,
M. Grumbacher, Inc.

Draw the head first with charcoal and indicate the shadows; dust the charcoal off if it is too heavy. The painting is then laid in with Burnt Sienna and a touch of Thalo* Blue. On the right, the head has been painted with a free stroke of the brush. The background is painted first, followed by the shadows, which are painted into the head to give form. The plate below shows the painting of the middle tones. The dark tones run into the background to give roundness. The brush is used freely and vigorously; all the white of the head is covered to give the tonal value of the flesh. The details of the eyes and brows are then rendered, followed by the nostrils and the mouth. The area below the head is allowed to remain the color of the background, thus directing all of the interest to the head.

* ® Reg. Trademark,
  M. Grumbacher, Inc.

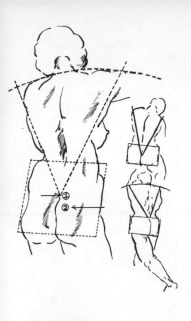

FORM

**Use of the triangle
and the square
as essential forms
for the back.**

From the shoulder to
the tuberosity of the
Sacrum ① we get a
triangle or wedge that
covers all of the back.
The Gluteus Maximus ②
is made in a square
or box shape.
This lets the torso move
in any direction.
Using the principle
of the wedge and the
square will give the
drawing a sound
and strong structure.

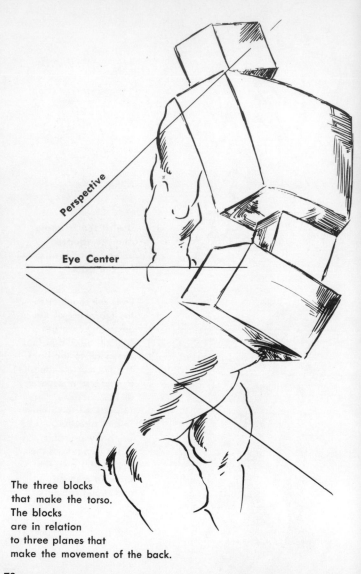

Perspective

Eye Center

The three blocks
that make the torso.
The blocks
are in relation
to three planes that
make the movement of the back.

Kobeck

It is well to think of the square for the major forms. Note how the square passes into the round form, and the wedging of the square into the distribution of all the masses of the figure.

John R. Grabach

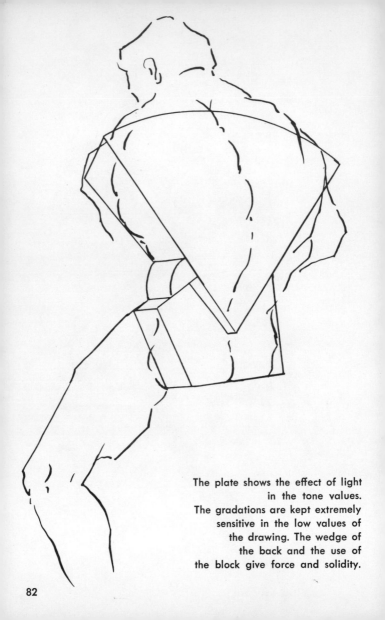

The plate shows the effect of light
in the tone values.
The gradations are kept extremely
sensitive in the low values of
the drawing. The wedge of
the back and the use of
the block give force and solidity.

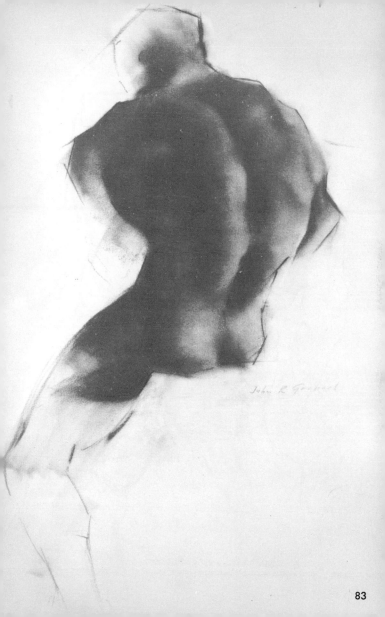

John R. Grabach

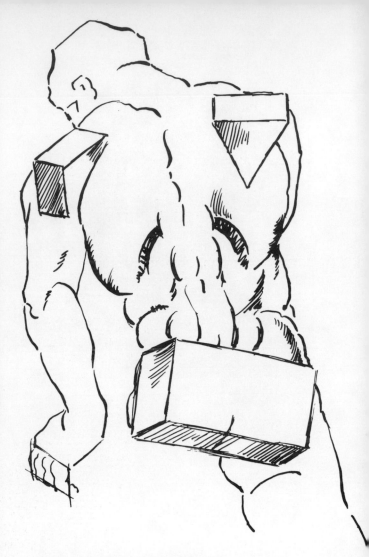

Masses showing the build-up of the back.

Use of the Angle

In this plate we see the use
of the angle throughout the figure.
The angle gives strength
as well as solidity.
This fundamental has been used
by such great artists
as Michelangelo and Hiroshige.

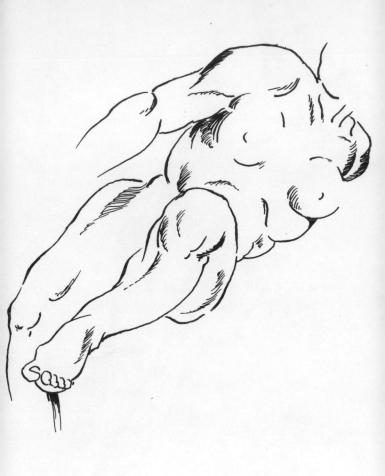

The change of position of
the leg when pulled up, representing
a foreshortened perspective.

John R Grabach

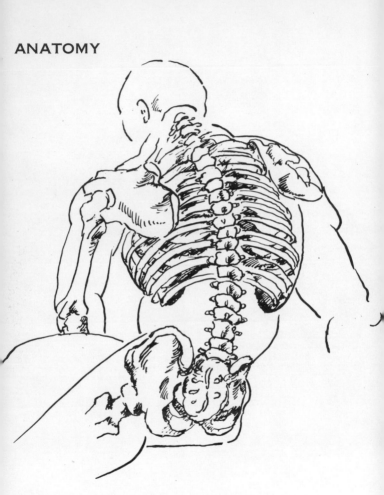

Skeleton of the back of drawing opposite.

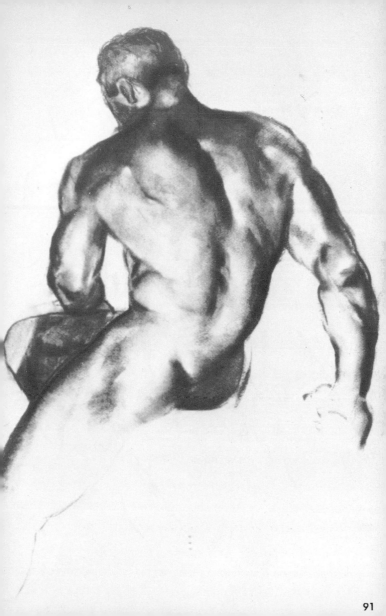

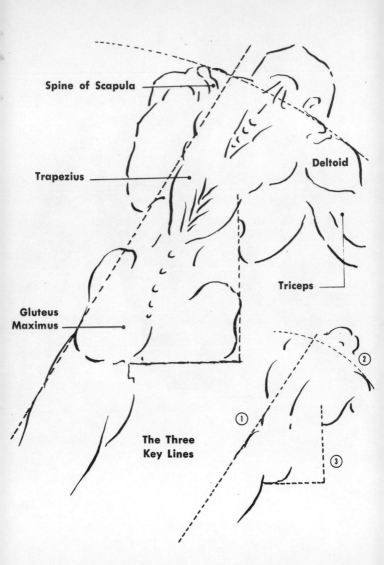

Spine of Scapula

Trapezius

Deltoid

Triceps

Gluteus
Maximus

The Three
Key Lines

① ② ③

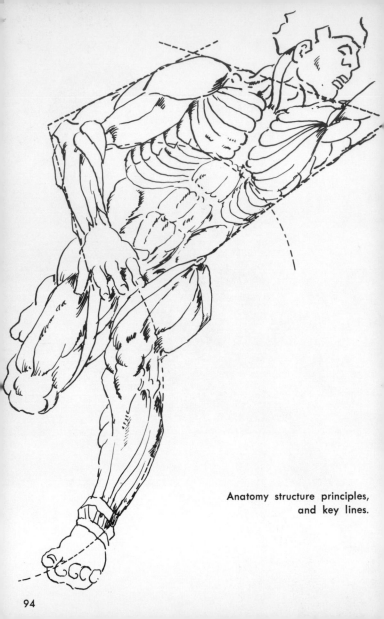

Anatomy structure principles,
and key lines.

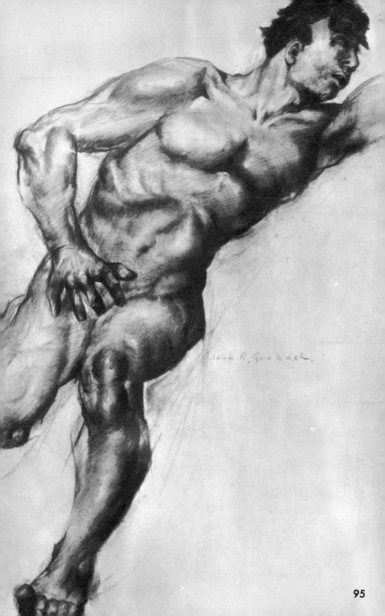

John R. Grabach,

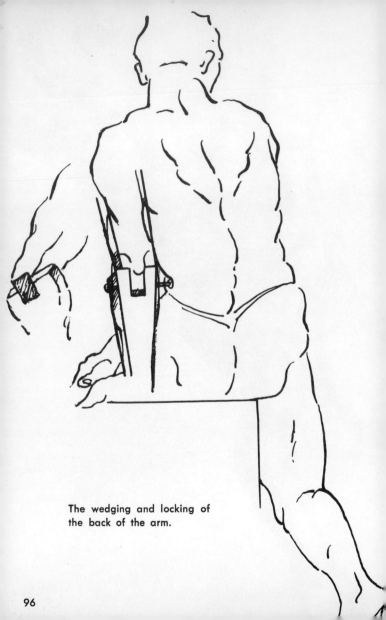

The wedging and locking of
the back of the arm.

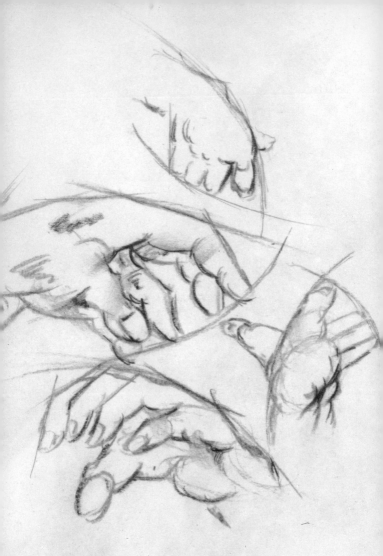

Showing the first spontaneous sketch
of hands on opposite page.

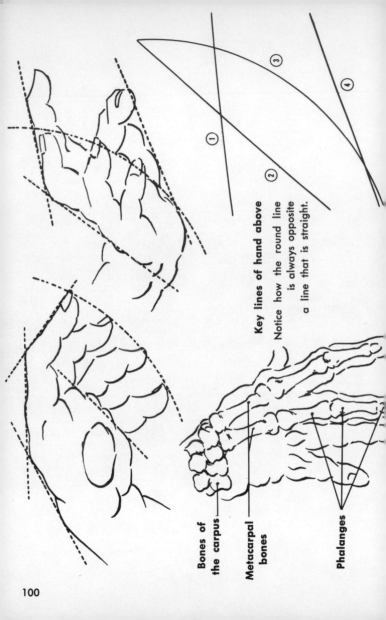

①

②

③

④

Key lines of hand above

Notice how the round line
is always opposite
a line that is straight.

Bones of
the carpus

Metacarpal
bones

Phalanges

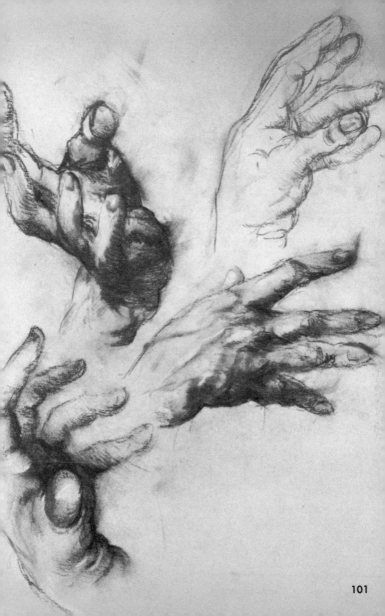

Key Lines in Composition

Importance of the key lines
in the composition
of the hands; notice how
the key lines take in all
the hands in the
composition. This applies
to figure groups
as well,
102 forming a design or unit.

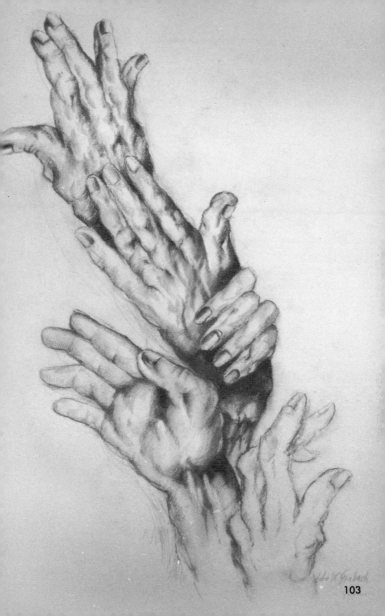

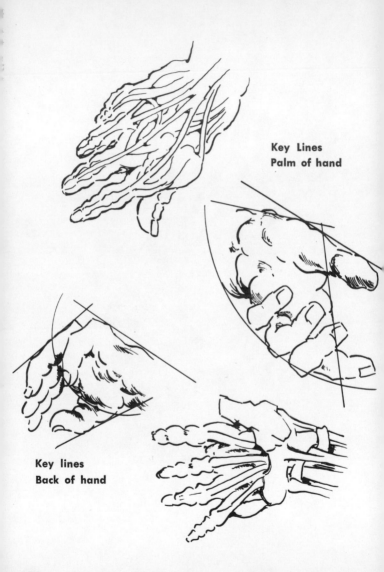

Key Lines
Palm of hand

Key lines
Back of hand

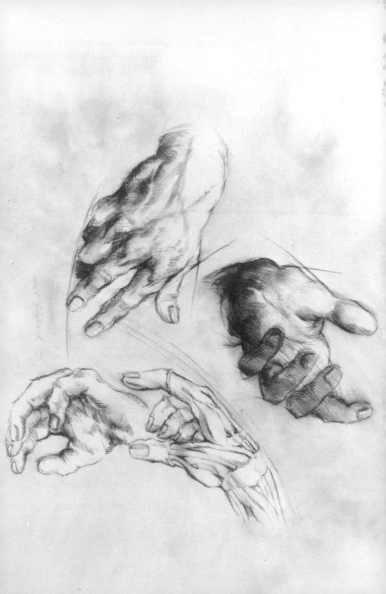

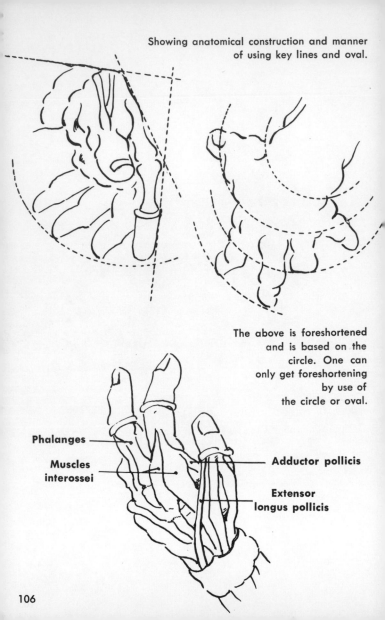

Showing anatomical construction and manner of using key lines and oval.

The above is foreshortened and is based on the circle. One can only get foreshortening by use of the circle or oval.

Phalanges

Muscles interossei

Adductor pollicis

Extensor longus pollicis

J S Grubach

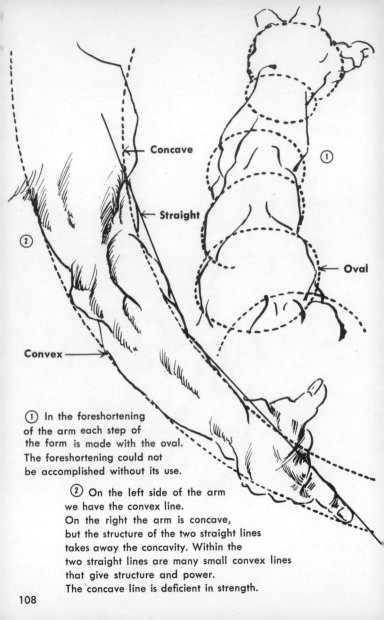

Concave

Straight

Oval

Convex

① In the foreshortening
of the arm each step of
the form is made with the oval.
The foreshortening could not
be accomplished without its use.

② On the left side of the arm
we have the convex line.
On the right the arm is concave,
but the structure of the two straight lines
takes away the concavity. Within the
two straight lines are many small convex lines
that give structure and power.
The concave line is deficient in strength.

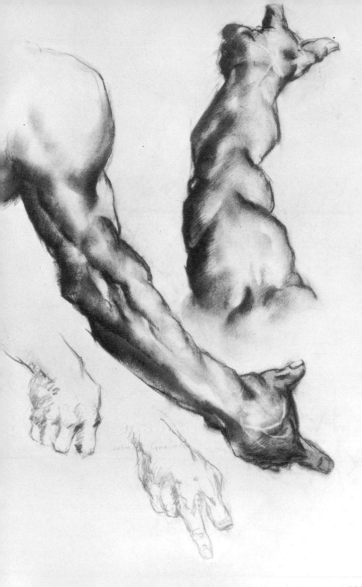

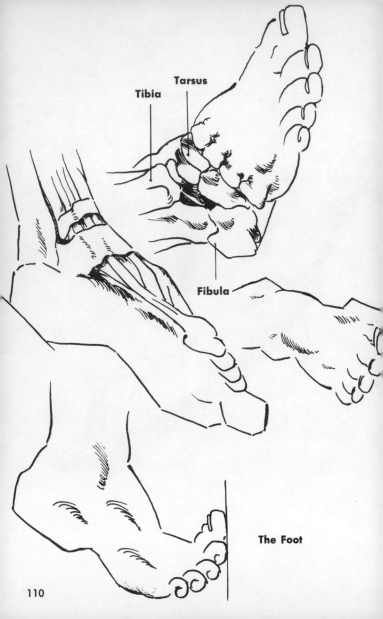

Tibia

Tarsus

Fibula

The Foot

110

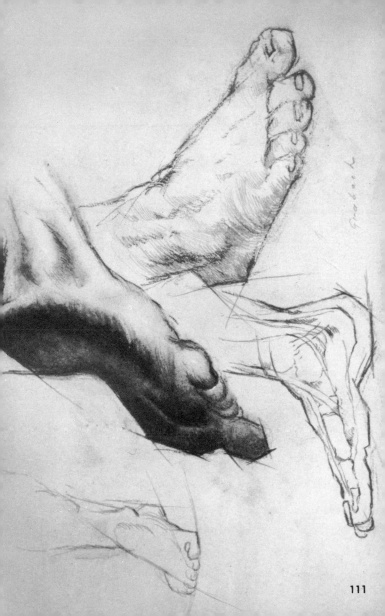

111

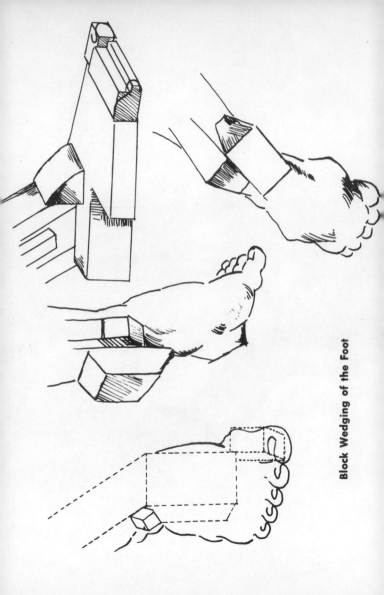

Block Wedging of the Foot

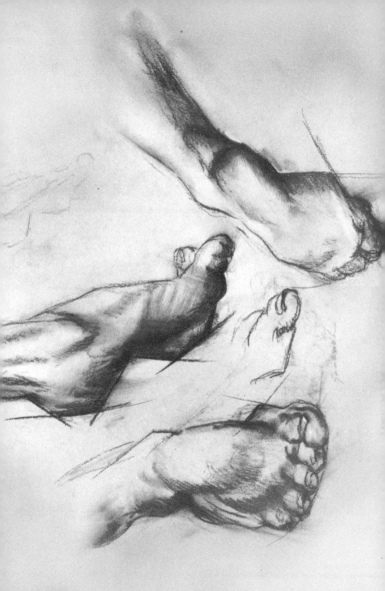

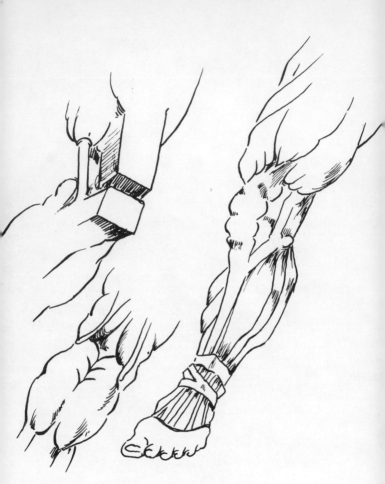

Wedge structure of the knee in action.

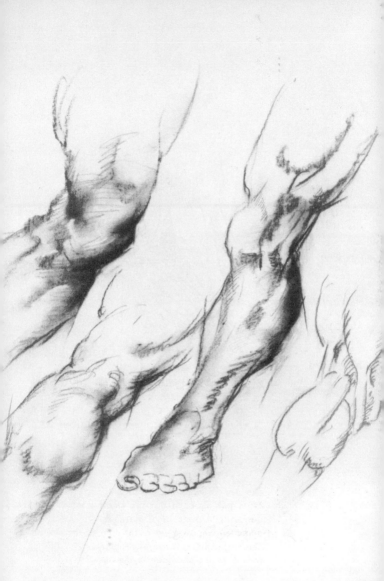

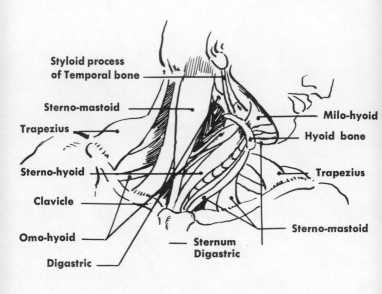

Styloid process
of Temporal bone

Sterno-mastoid

Trapezius

Sterno-hyoid

Clavicle

Omo-hyoid

Digastric

Milo-hyoid

Hyoid bone

Trapezius

Sterno-mastoid

Sternum
Digastric

The neck is a cylindrical shape.
From behind each ear the sterno-mastoid
descends to the root of the neck,
and they almost meet each other at the sternum.
The trapezius, a large back muscle,
rolls over the shoulder to the neck.

Study of the Neck

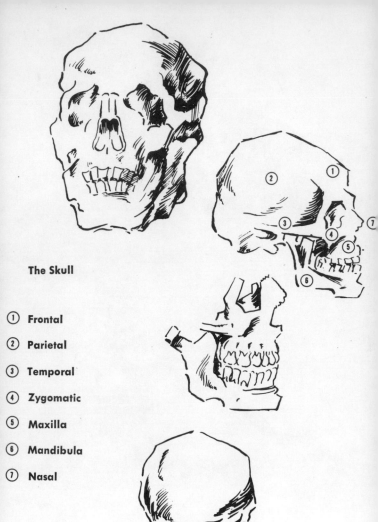

The Skull

1. **Frontal**
2. **Parietal**
3. **Temporal**
4. **Zygomatic**
5. **Maxilla**
6. **Mandibula**
7. **Nasal**

118

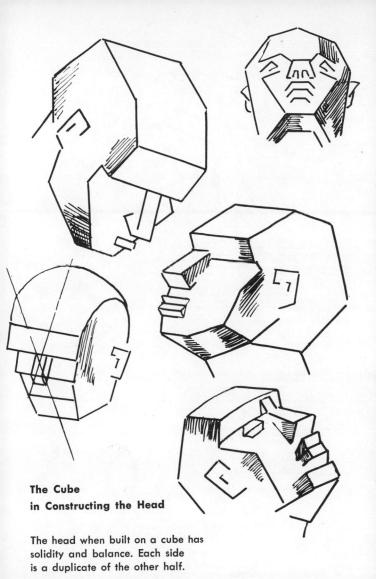

The Cube
in Constructing the Head

The head when built on a cube has
solidity and balance. Each side
is a duplicate of the other half.

Planes of the Head

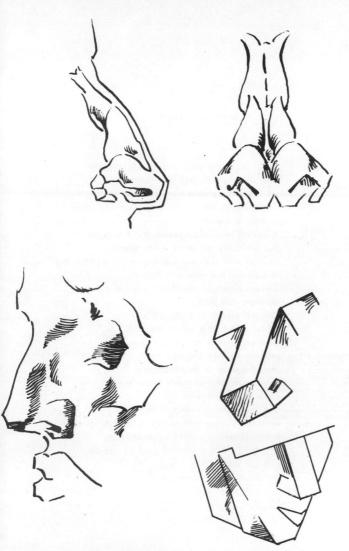

Nose Structure

SILVER POINT

Used as early as the sixteenth century,
the silver point was a favorite
of the old masters for sketching.
The metallic lead originally used
is now a piece of
graphite lead, sharpened to a fine point.
An ordinary piece of white paper
coated with Chinese white and allowed to dry
is best for the purpose, though
certain types of art paper carried by most
dealers will serve.
Glazed paper is preferable.
Silver point is a direct method,
and erasure is practically impossible
without ruining the drawing.
The drawing is accomplished
by the placing of many close lines
covering the figure.
Use the natural swing of the hand.
In adding the form keep to the original lines,
being careful to cross none of them.
A regular lead pencil of medium grade
can be substituted
for the metallic lead.

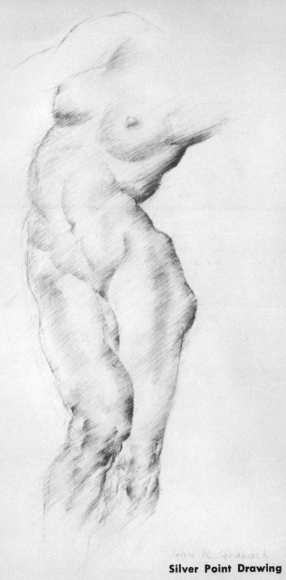

John R. Grabach

Silver Point Drawing

John R Grabach

Silver Point Drawing

Silver Point Drawing

BLACK PAPER DRAWINGS

This drawing is made on black paper
with very soft, black charcoal
and white chalk. The charcoal is blacker
than the paper, and consequently can be seen.
The drawing is first laid out
with the charcoal, after which the white chalk
is used for the light portions.
It is best not to rub the chalk with the fingers;
rubbing the white will make it
lose its quality and look hard. The
beauty of the drawing comes from having
the tooth of the paper show.
The white should be used sparingly.
Too heavy application will produce
unattractive results. Use of black with
the white on the paper gives
value to the drawing, making it less harsh.
The drawing can be sprayed
with fixative, or with Tuffilm ™* Spray Fixative
as can any charcoal drawing.
Keep about eighteen inches away with the
first spraying. After the chalk and charcoal
have been partially fixed you can
get closer, but if you are too close
on the first spraying, it will
blow away too much of the loose chalk.

*Trademark of M. Grumbacher, Inc.

On Gray Paper

Structure is indicated
by slight variations of tone

129

DRAPERY

The fabric of all drapery will produce
folds of distinctive character.
Heavy drapery will have the oval and never
the angle; silk will have the angle
and also the oval.
Heavy drapery has a slow line; cotton
or silk will have a fast line.
The twisting of folds always makes spirals and
acute angles or ovals. In studying
the character of drapery keep in mind the
difference in the relationship of the materials.
Weight and texture will have much to do
with movement and speed of the folds.
Some folds will be straight, festooned or V-shaped;
folds will fall, cross, or pass each other.
Each drapery has its own laws;
each must be studied as a fixed law and linked
to others in a rhythm. Only the details of
these laws vary. Much depends
upon the material used.
The manner of drawing drapery has
varied during different art periods.
The Gothic used more of the angle than the
oval line, while the Renaissance period
used both the angle and the round line.
The Greeks used long flowing lines
terminating in the angle or the oval.

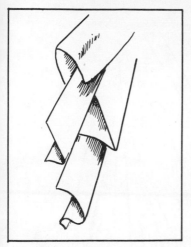

Gothic

Renaissance

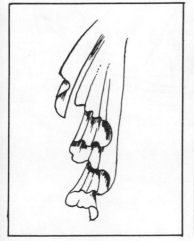

Greek

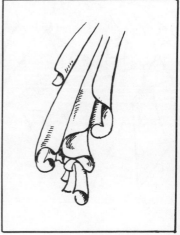

Greek

Angle

Showing the use of the angle
that is swift in its movement.

John R. Grabach

Angle and Oval

How angle and oval
are combined.

Oval

Showing the use of the oval.

136

137

JOHN R. GRABACH is a native of Massachusetts. He studied painting and drawing at the Art Students League in New York, and with George B. Bridgman, Frank V. DuMond, Kenyon Cox and H. Augustus Schwabe. For more than twenty years he has been an instructor at the Newark (New Jersey) School of Fine and Industrial Arts. He has taught life drawing, figure and landscape painting to more than 4,000 students, many of whom have become well-known artists.

Among others Mr. Grabach has won the Peabody Prize of the Art Institute of Chicago, the Susan Gold Medal of the Pennsylvania Academy of the Fine Arts, and the Preston Harrison Prize of the Los Angeles Museum. He has had one-man shows at the Art Institute of Chicago, the Grand Central Galleries in New York, the Memorial Art Gallery of Rochester, New York, and the Irvington (New Jersey) Art and Museum Association, of which he was also a Director. Grabach drawings and paintings now hang in the Art Institute of Chicago, the Corcoran Gallery, the International Business Machines Gallery, and in other public and numerous private collections. He has participated in group shows in New York, Washington, Pittsburgh, Toledo, San Francisco, St. Louis, Louisville, Richmond, Indianapolis, Buffalo and Detroit.